**ANCHOR BOOKS**

TWIST IN THE TALE

Edited by

Sarah Andrew

First published in Great Britain in 2002 by
ANCHOR BOOKS
Remus House,
Coltsfoot Drive,
Peterborough, PE2 9JX
Telephone (01733) 898102

HB ISBN 1 85930 994 1
SB ISBN 1 85930 999 2

FOREWORD

Anchor Books is a small press, established in 1992, with the aim of promoting readable poetry to as wide an audience as possible.

We hope to establish an outlet for writers of poetry who may have struggled to see their work in print.

The poems presented here have been selected from many entries. Editing proved to be a difficult task and as the Editor, the final selection was mine.

I trust this selection will delight and please the authors and all those who enjoy reading poetry.

Sarah Andrew
Editor

While Grandmother Waited

written by

Susan Carole Roberts

on page 48

CONTENTS

THE OTHER WOMAN

The other woman's sleek and smart and always up to date,
While I am somewhat dowdy, trying not to hate
The grace and beauty even I,
Her foremost rival, can't deny.
I know too well her hold on him, I understand her charm and guile,
For even when he's with me I see that distant smile,
And know she's in his thoughts again,
He speaks of her with eyes aglow,
And if his fondness brings me pain,
That's something I don't let him know,
For how can I compare with her? She's perfect in so many ways,
Every time he speaks of her I'll hear him sing her praise,
Even when he speaks of love
And holds me in his arms,
A part of him is yearning
For her and all her charms,
Too soon he'll be returning,
I must share him with her other love, a jealous mistress she,
Who lures him far away across the wide blue sea,
Her hull is sleek and smart,
Her sails as white as snow,
Although it breaks my heart,
I have to let him go,
His hand is on the tiller, the hand that once held mine,
He'll feel her move to his command with pride his eyes will shine,
So who am I to hold him here? I just wait by the shore,
Until the other woman brings him back to me once more!

Ailsa Keen

TOGETHERNESS

You have been my partner now for just a little while
But in that short time you have taught me how to smile
The year before I met you, I had been in such awful pain,
And I was so depressed I thought I'd never be happy again.

I really was an emotional wreck when you came to visit me
I was actually agoraphobic and as scared as scared could be.
But we became such good friends, we just clicked right away,
That I couldn't live without you, I need you more each day.

We go out together every day and I'm not scared anymore
So different from when I used to hide and not go to the door.
I've made so many new friends and I go out to meet them too
My confidence increases daily and all because of you.

I've even learned to laugh again and I never get depressed
You even bring my clothes to help me when I'm getting dressed
As you have moved in to live with me which gives me so
                                        much pleasure.
Each day we have new adventures and memories to treasure.

You are so beautiful with your silky golden hair
My life is now complete again as you are always there
You lavish love and care on me . . . I am the lucky receiver
My friend . . . my confidante . . . my eyes . . . my lovely
                                        golden retriever.

Mary Anne Scott

INEVITABLE FRIEND

Sadly he came at the dead of night
when searching winds blew cold
and scarce was any clear sky
tinged with frost's blue light
unseen by all, not even patrolling
searching owl.

He came silently attentive as
a stray dog out on a night's prowl
even double glazed secured windows
and door could not hold him back
from his determined pursuit
his mission by passing time itself
faster now he treads then a sigh,
a blink, even breath itself.

But thankfully sleep was the saviour
for this poor man
when he was taken, chosen
by no one's inevitable friend . . .
death.

Roy Wootton

LISTENING IN!

'Can you hear me, Mother?
I'm on the radio;
You'll have to turn the sound up loud,
Then me voice you'll surely know!
It's your Billy, Mother,
I'm having quite a treat,
'Cos they brought us lads together,
As was playin' down our street!

Can yer hear me, Mother?
Shout up if yer can:
As a sed, I'm on the radio;
They've got it in a van.
There's a nice chap 'ere in uniform,
Sez 'e's monit'rin fer sound,
And if you'd like a licence,
'E'll be pleased ter bring one round . . .

So . . .
If you can hear me, Mother,
Talking on the radio,
Just come an' draw our curt'ns back
Ter let this nice man know.
If yer look out through the winder,
Yer'll see the van outside,
An' 'e sez that when 'e comes again,
'E'll tek us fer a ride!

Can yer hear me, Mother?
I think I've got to go;
'E sez somethin' 'bout I've blown it,
Now ev'ryone will know!
Can yer 'ear me, Mother? I think it's goin' faint;
Oh! 'E's pulled the plug! Am I stoppin'? No, I ain't!'

Bee Wickens

FORGIVE ME

My life's companion for fifteen years or more,
Outlasting sleeker rivals, long gone before,
You remain at my side, never wavering.

You rarely see my better moods or actions
And sadly routine are the small attentions
Delivered your way by these unfeeling hands.

But note, you are also not beyond reproof.
My world of fantasy you cruelly encroach
And drag me back to life's stern reality.

I'm caught on a treadmill and it starts with you.
I seize you with force, hate igniting anew.
But oh! the remorse for the hurt inflicted.

And now, my head full of screwdrivers drilling,
I return home finding you're hoarse with shrilling,
I'll switch you off next time; dear clock, forgive me!

Margaret Gregory

BLISS

I can choose from a hammock or sunbed
A lounger, a deckchair or stool;
Spend an hour by the flowerbeds watching them grow
Or relax, in the shade, by the pool.

For breakfast, fresh fruit and a coffee,
Now dinner is sent when I call:
I can dream up the most tempting menus and meals
As I'm doing no cooking at all.

Lethargic, I lean by the fish pond.
Look, even the fish are asleep,
All glossy and sleek as the new magazines
Lying there by my chair in a heap.

That alarm clock is unplugged and silent,
Unwatched while I idle and yawn.
Slow as ice cubes that melt in my lemon and lime
Time slides by, and I doze on the lawn.

'Half your luck! Can I join you?' You're saying,
'I too would be happy to shirk.'
As for me, I'll be glad when my broken leg heals
And at last I can go back to work.

Vivien Butters

I SHOULDN'T HAVE SAID IT

I shouldn't have said that I would soon be found out
But when she was talking I just wanted to shout
When I met Mrs Smith with her long stories she would greet
We would meet when out shopping down our busy street
When she spoke of her family it was told with great pride
They climbed such tall mountains and from rough seas wouldn't hide
Of course they went flying and the fastest jets they always took
Her young brother was now writing another long book
My own cousin wrote poetry I managed to state
And when one was printed it was given a high rate
My bus was now coming so nothing more I would say
But I knew we would meet up some other day
Next week Mrs Smith had plans for what I had said
And some special meeting was thought out in her head
Her friends all now wanted this new poet to meet
She would read them her poems what a wonderful treat
I shouldn't have said that, what a daft thing to do
But I wouldn't deny it because it was true
Jane's poem wasn't special as all folk would know
Somewhere on the woman's page it might be put on show
When having hair done this rhyme was thought of by Jane one day
She sent these few lines where the spray was being sold
The owners seemed to like how the story was told
So they sent her six bottles and there was nothing to spend
But could each one be sent to her own special friend
How Mrs Smith should get these poems read with pride
But a scribble of six lines was all I could provide
I shouldn't have said it now I am really found out
And as for Mrs Smith I knew she would shout.

May Walker

THE UNWANTED COMPANION

'Run faster, run faster!'
　My heart beats like a drum,
I know deep inside I must win this race.
　Something daunting runs behind me,
keeping to the shadows,
　these eyes never see its face.

'It is there, my soul knows it is there!'
　Panic grips my mind,
filling every inch of my body with fear.
　'Who are you?' 'What are you?'
These words are spoken in silence,
　in case something awful should appear.

'Did I fall asleep so quickly,
　allowing the thing to enter my dreams?'
Once again fear rips at my soul.
　Like an animal it haunts me,
watching from the distance,
　standing in the darkness longing to take control.

I search for somewhere to hide,
　somewhere safe, somewhere warm,
a room with a locked door.
　Still the thing gets closer,
my legs are growing weaker,
　soon I will be unable to run anymore.

'It is here, my tormentor!'
　Darkness closes around me,
at last my pursuer catches his prey.
　Loneliness arrives like a curse,
the most evil of evils,
　destined to be my companion by night and day.

M A Challis

INESCAPABLE

As we release ourselves from this moment,
This vision is ours to be discovered,
Wishful thoughts to interpret
Fragile hearts explode emotions to imagine.
In this darkness through this life
Capture spirits in this element
Through the light surrender beauty refined.
Desperate soul secluding my forbidden destiny.

Angela Giles

TOAD PRINCESS

Young Prince Reynaud
came trotting down the road
in the middle of which
was seated - a forlorn toad

As he commenced to ride on by
he was startled - when
he thought he heard it cry

'Please, young sir
don't leave me this way
I was a fair young princess
in some - long, distant day.'

An evil warlock - wanted us betrothed
to be lover (I refused)
so he turned me into this loathsome load

He dismounted beside her
'That was an ungallant thing to do
my name is Prince Reynaud
how can I be of assistance to you.

'For me to become human again,
you must do this
(puckering her lips) - give me a kiss.'

'Young Prince - be brave, kiss me if you dare.'
The gallant one - did as he was bode
the transformation - instantaneous
in front of him, a princess not a toad.

'Sorry Prince - who said life was fair!'
She mounted his horse - rode away
leaving behind a sad, bewildered toad croaking there.

Rod Palmer

WISHFUL THINKING

The thoughtless demon before he's caught,
By the wizened witch with whiskered wart,
Tries so hard to be cruel but nice.
Like eating cake while clamped in a vice.
Leans on a stick that's gnarled and old,
Poking his pile of worthless gold.
His thin moustache and v-shaped hair
Glisten with grease in the moonlit air
Juggling jewels that appear so rare,
Into the moonlight's garish glare.
He spies the old witch with eyebrow raised
Peers at her like a man half crazed.
Lifts his stick to assail the hag
Arrested by a spell from her well worn bag.
Stopped in his tracks, he becomes enraged
Lunges forth as a lion encaged.
Imprisoned quick as a lightning flash
Suffers strokes of the witch's long lash.
He lies in torment, cold and starved
Trussed up like a bird to be cooked and carved.
He sits in the corner of his cold damp cell
Thinking of paradise, nice warm hell.

Andrew Handsaker

THE DRIP

It started with a little drip, every now and then,
It had always been this way, since can't remember when.

Just a little nuisance, that we pushed from our minds,
A kind of lazy habit, when things like this we find.

Then the drip, became a plop, much louder than before,
So we could not hear it, we chose to shut the door.

These nagging little globlets, with monotony did fall,
No one took much notice, of this minute waterfall.

The plop then turned into a splash, water spreading out,
Not one serious look it got, we were always out.

The splash became a constant flow, destined not to stop,
Some poor demented tenant, had hit it on the top.

The tap all rough and dented, looked a sorry state,
And on the fed up lodgers, this noise began to grate.

This dripping, plopping, splashing, flowing, aggravating mess,
Was given all the tenants, a load of blinking stress.

Then one day, it reared its head, and bought us all to book,
As we entered in the hall, we just amazed did look.

For down the stairs, a waterfall, was streaming at full speed,
This kind of major aggro, we really didn't need.

Everybody panicked, and reached for bowl and mop,
Through the swirling waters, 'cause the tap was at the top.

No one begged to volunteer, to wade up to the source,
We phoned the local plumber, to this mess, of course.

Spanner furled, and bag of tools, he beaver'ed on to help us fools,
As tenants, we should have known the rules.

A nice fat cheque was ours to pay, it landed on the mat.
If we'd changed the washer, it wouldn't have come to that.

When dealing with a mighty force, remember one small drip,
Can grow into an endless surge, and make the house a tip.

Duchess Newman

BALLISTIC!

The lady greeted Jim warmly, her washer to repair
Through the hall, to the lounge, she guided him there
Her infant son, on the floor with his toys
Was happily playing the game of young boys
As Jim passed through, he just couldn't resist
Kicking a ball, as the boy's mother hissed
The impact was hard, off the TV it bounced
She went ballistic, and verbally pounced
'Lady,' Jim pleaded, 'there's no harm done
The TV's undamaged, I just kicked it for fun.'
She shrieked and wailed, it took a full minute
To realise her concern - the hamster was in it!

Mary Wood

THE SOUL ORCHARD

Soul columns suited in skin
staring at these gilded edges of death
craved open like flesh
rectangle and raw.
Immortal as daylight
in this orchard of graves
as washing line breath whiff
pegged mind frames
rattling autumn lungs
at the soil cradle.
Knuckle still in the clasping chill
licked by flames
inevitable wounds whistle
into the furnace of dreams.

J R Griffiths

ABANDONED

Once it was me and you,
Against the world, just us two,
I was number one in your eyes,
And was your most treasured prize,
But you changed as I grew older
You wanted something younger and bolder,
I just didn't know what to do,
As I still thought the world of you.

Then onto the scene she came,
Life for me then was never quite the same,
We never went out so much,
Eventually we just lost touch.
You even passed me onto your friend,
But I didn't suit his image or trend,
One night when we were supposed to meet,
He didn't turn up, leaving me alone in a deserted street,

I have been here for ages now, nobody seems to care,
Life can be cruel sometimes also quite unfair,
Now I am on the scrapheap,
It really makes me want to weep,
Everyone has had a piece of me as well,
And now I am just an empty shell,
But in my memory it has left a scar,
Me, I am just an abandoned car.

Maureen Arnold

A CASE OF ABUSE

I'm sought out to cater for comfort
A treasure to pleasure your ease.
Yet I'm jumped on and thoroughly pummelled
Plus anything else that you please

I give in designed for a purpose
Adorn 'til I'm worn to a thread,
Yet you throw me and stuff in the corner
Ashamed to display me instead

But still, I'm your friend when you're wilting
With cuddles to show me you care,
I'm a softie you can't live without me,
That cushion in your favourite chair.

Sam Royce

A Peep At Nature's Treasure House

When we look, do we truly see those sparkling dewdrops on the
grass, nature's diamonds glistening in the early morning sunlight?

We pause only for a moment to draw a quick breath at the sight
of an azure carpet of bluebells in a sun-dappled wood.

Have we really studied the symmetry of a glistening jet-black
blackberry growing among its half-ripe fellows?

What of the copper-tinted leaves we see in a wood in autumn,
drifting down noiselessly into the brown bracken below?

The earthy smell and soft texture of mushroom caps that suddenly
appear overnight. What mysterious hand wills them to appear?

Have we paused and marvelled at the wonderful delicacy of a
cobweb, the equi-distant strands rotated around a centre spot -
the whole web suspended maybe, between gatepost and a shrub?

Have we really studied the honeybee's handiwork, that
wonderful construction the honeycomb? No need of slide rule
or template, it is perfectly formed.

The white silence of falling snow which blots out the
ugly angles of buildings and broken fences and dulls
unpleasant sounds.

We should look and listen a little more closely at
the treasure house which surrounds us.
By whose hand?
God has bestowed on us all the guardianship of
His treasure house.

Hilary M Andrews

A FISHY TALE OF A TWIST IN TIME

A heron in search of a morsel of food,
Swooped down on a small garden pond,
Clipped tight in her beak a slim sliver of gold
Then soared up and sped into beyond.

The morsel, so outraged, just wriggled and squirmed,
Escaped and fell down into space,
Helplessly dropped to a grim fishy end
But survived as a newspaper case.

'Fish fell down a chimney, to bounce off the coals
Onto hearth and lie motionless, frail,
But alerted by daughter, a mother just gazed,
Then the fish gave a flick of its tail.

Quickly the creature was put in a bowl
For a life saving shot in the fin.
RSPCA help came to rescue that fish,
Which now swims with its own kith and kin'.

One can only but marvel that people so cared
For the life of a little goldfish,
But consider the plight of the heron in flight
If it cannot find fish for its dish.

Pat Squire

GROWING PAINS

With pride I've watch my grandson
grow to over six foot tall
I'd dreamed he'd 'take up' medicine
or hear some noble call.

I know he has a safe retreat
to share with teenage friends,
loud music and funny jokes
an exchange of modern trends.

One day I was more than curious
refreshments I took to share,
but oh! His new found love stood
stripped right down and bare!

It's not for me to judge if
talent lies in his hands,
a pre-conceived genetic force
has scuppered well laid plans.

I'm trusting he will ponder as
he renews his piston rings,
and know his bike was but an object
in a quest of greater things.

Olive Bedford

My First Trip Abroad

I'm all of a dither,
I'm excited and scared,
We're off on a journey together,
It's my first trip,
I think we're off,
But it all depends on the weather.

My brothers and sisters are going as well,
Mum 'n' Dad've been before.
I hope I don't let the side down,
I really don't know the score.

We'll go up in the clouds
In the clear blue sky,
Over the mountains and sea
O what a view we'll have
- I've been told -
If I'm good as good as can be.

I hope I'll be able to stay awake
And not fall asleep on the way
Cos I'll miss such a lot
Of the things we shall see
And I don't want to lose my way!

Mum says it's great,
We'll have lots of fun,
But we'll be back on the loose!
Back to my playground
With all my mates!
Just another Canadian Goose.

Hilary Vint

DINGLEY DELL

At eventide again he takes
  The downward path through Dingley Dell
A lovely, but secluded spot,
  Its isolation serves him well

And yet he feels disquietude
  A faint fey prickling in his hair,
The reason for this vague unease
  An emanation in the air;

An odour, as of fresh-turned soil
  And putrefaction, sickly sweet,
Accelerates his shrinking heart
  And fetters his reluctant feet

For there, upon the shadowed path,
  A ghastly apparition forms,
Again he sees the bloodstained head
  Now blurred with residue of worms.

In vain he begs deliverance
  But naught he'll do can break the spell
Of the figure reaching for him, which
  He'd buried, deep in Dingley Dell.

J C Fearnley

HOMEWORK - THE POEM

One day my teacher said to me:
'For homework write some poetry.'
I went home feeling rather sad
But then I thought, 'I'll ask my dad!'
He said, 'What's the matter son -
You seem to be looking a wee bit glum?'
I said, 'I've got to write a poem.'
'Oh dear,' said Dad, 'I must be going!'
'But Dad!' I sighed, 'I need your help please.'
'OK Son, but to me poetry doesn't come with ease,
First let me think of a rhyming word -'
Dad sat down, the cat yawned and purred
Dad stroked the head of our old cat
As she lay curled up on the mat.
Dad and I thought of words galore
Then he decided it was getting a bore
I couldn't think of what to write
I glanced at Dad - he'd given up the fight
He'd gone to sleep in his chair
I said aloud, 'Oh, this isn't fair!
Wake up Dad and please help me -
I've got to do this poetry!'
Eventually I wrote this poem
About my dad without him knowing!

Lynne Done

HEART'S DESIRE

The fire was burning big and bright,
The wind was howling loud that night.
I settled down by the roaring fire -
Thinking of my heart's desire.
Although it was by chance we'd met,
In the waiting room of the village vet.

By now I was feeling cosy and warm,
Oblivious to the noisy storm.
My thoughts drifted back to events of the day,
How my friend and I ran through fields of hay.
Running and jumping - so good for the soul.
Watching a rabbit scamper down a small hole.

There were birds on the fence singing a song,
But when we ran over - they were soon gone,
Flying up high - they were laughing at us,
As if they were saying, 'What's all the fuss?'
Soon it was time to go back to our home,
Too tired out now to further roam.

The wind was still howling - then a voice outside
Made me sit up and look for somewhere to hide
For the voice that I heard was coming my way.
Closer and closer - oh what would he say?
Because I was sat on my friend's favourite chair,
He'd probably say, 'What are you doing there'?

As he came through the door - my eyes opened wide,
For my heart's desire ran up to my side.
Puffing and panting - pink tongue poking out,
She's the one in the vet's I'd been thinking about.
The storm was over and no longer alone,
The two of us sharing a huge doggy bone!

Christine M Tracey

A View From The Window

He stood in the sun's bright ray,
He stood there every single day.
Sunshine was his just reward,
It was all he could afford.

He stood alone throughout the year,
He stood there in mortal fear.
In fear of what? He only knew,
In his mind, a different view.

He knew the view would be the same,
He always played this childish game.
Imagining a different scene,
If only! It had never been.

His life was simply purgatory,
Hence his sad life story.
The window was high on the cell wall,
The view was no view at all.

The poor prisoner in his cell,
Had no view about which to tell.
Only a picture on the wall,
Was better than no view at all.

So ends my tale of a missing view,
So is the sad little story true?
If it is, the captive lies,
For he is blind, he has no eyes!

Mick Butcher

WHEN LOVELY WOMAN STOOPS

My childhood outside Cheltenham was idyllic,
With lots of time for play and lots for knowledge,
Brownies and ballet, interests zoophilic,
Ponies, gymkhanas - then on to Ladies College.

The dream continued, blissful, bucolic, balmy -
House Captain, dux, eurhythmic dancing (Dorian,)
Gold cups for elocution, origami,
Latin and Greek, then school valedictorian.

Vacations were equivalently yummy -
Long interludes in Bruges, Biarritz and Venice,
The Uffizi and the Boboli with Mummy,
On Daddy's yacht - then Wimbledon for tennis.

So on to Christ Church for the autumn term -
Moral Philosophy, Classics and Theology.
My cashmere twin set and my brand new perm
Inflamed a Wykehamist with interests in Biology

Who introduced me to alternative psychology -
Object: attainment of divine nirvana,
À la Blavatskyesque theosophy,
Induced through LSD or marijuana,

Cocaine or crack, preceding lots of sex.
Enlightenment came late - and with a sense of loss.
Tune in, chill out, and join the human wrecks.
Right now I'm turning tricks around King's Cross.

Norman Bissett

COLOURS

Palest pink, like a delicate rose,
Turns lilac and blue, as it grows,
Every day are different hues.
As it deepens, to reds and blues.
Later, there are shades of yellow,
With dark purple to follow.
Would anyone choose,
To have a painful bruise?

Joan Williams

DOWNFALL

How you thrill me, fascinate me
With your flashing eyes so bright
When I see you I long for you
But this wanting I must fight.

I need to caress your smooth body
Though I know I should not dare
'Cause once more you'll be my downfall
This is a hopeless love affair.

Yet I know I can't resist you
You appeal so much to me!
And I try, myself to distance
As far away as I could be.

But, oh Lord, this urge to touch you
Is ingrained in me so strong
And I vow, this'll be the last time
Then I never shall go wrong!

Quickly I reach into my pocket
And one by one, coins I put in
Till the last of them are swallowed
Into the big, bright slot machine.

Of course, again, I am the loser
Stony broke, my wanting purged
Deep inside, I know I must stop
I can't stay a slave to this urge!

Yet, the thought of bright lights flashing
And quick riches jangling out
Turns my knees weak, my heart thumping
And resolutions gets thrown out.

So yet again, the road to ruin
Beckons me to press once more
Those bright coloured, magic buttons
That brings my downfall, like before.

M Ellerton

It Was A Wild And Windy Night

It was a wild and windy night
Thirty foot waves on the bird bath,
And a distinct slop in the fish kettle.
Enough to be more than a little uncomfortable, Foam
Boiling up, as the water sloshed
Through the holes in the platform.

Not a night to brave the elements.
Intrepid but no Captain Ahab.

The wind burped through the rigging
Unsettling his duck, perched
A figurehead on the soap dish.
Well, maybe he will turn in
For the night and wait for the morrow to
Cast off
His one pearl and two plain
Fisherman's knit.

Jack Major

METAMORPHOSIS

She has transformed me with her rage:
Into a toad,
Symbol of all things loathsome
And blackly magical.
She denounces me as:
The Prince of Darkness,
Paederast, wife beater,
Promoter of porn and snuff films,
Drug dealer and murderer –
Even multi-millionaire.
And how my heart is saddened by
Her scornful fury,
Her assault on all the things
She knows I hold hateful.
Yet there must be better times –
I have just had the four 'worse' I vowed to accept
When we married all those years ago.
Then, she will smile at me in the morning,
Hold my hand, stroke my back as she passes my chair,
Offer me tea, though little sympathy,
Give indications of her loving
And, because I crave love,
I will roll over and pant for more.
For that is the real metamorphosis:
My love for her has turned me into her pet pup,
Devoid of pride and anger,
Willing for the kicking.

Ted Harriott

Upheaval

I've lived here now for several years
Peaceful and busy but having no fears
Small interruptions now and again
When a gust of wind would disturb my den
Then all of a sudden out of the blue
Came bangs and clatters, such hullabaloo
Moving of objects - the scattering of dust
The sweeping and brushing and I know that I must
Keep out of the way of that duster and broom
Disaster has to come to my once quiet room
I watched as my home disappeared from my sight
With a flick of the wrist - and I scuttled with fright
The hours I'd spent weaving finest of threads
And then came the moment that everyone dreads
Spring cleaning - and nothing was safe any more
I hurriedly scamper across the clean floor
Soon all will be clean and I'll then have begun
To stretch silken threads which will gleam in the sun
An intricate pattern - delightful to spy
But fatal attraction to entrap the fly
For spiders are patient and wily and sly
They're more than a match for the silly old fly
So we'll carry on life in the very same way
Until the next time there comes the dread day
Of the duster and brush, the water and mop
Once started she never knows when she should stop
So I hope that again I'll have a long rest
Before I'm disturbed by that spring cleaning zest.

Kath Barber

NEIGHBOURS FROM HELL

Just a minute Mrs Jones, I really must protest
Your noisy all night parties are leaving me depressed
My nerves are getting shattered, my temper's wearing thin
If this goes on much longer, I'll call the coppers in.

I thought I'd have an early night, so I curled up in my bed
It seemed a herd of elephants were stamping overhead
The cracks upon the ceiling have spread a little more
Your guests have yet to learn it seems, the way to shut a door.

I fell asleep exhausted, then woke up in a fright
As one by one, outside my door, they shouted out 'Goodnight'
The noise they made on leaving, was really quite absurd
Only to be rivalled by the singing of the birds.

'I can't stand it Mrs Jones, it's like the third degree
So when you throw the next one
Will you please ask me!'

Milly Hatcher

NOT NOW DEAR

Can we go swimming Mummy please?
Not now dear, not today
No time for that now when
There's clothes to iron and things to mend

Can we go to the swings Mummy please?
Not now, another time we may
I'm far too busy doing things
Cleaning the house and telephoning

Can we go to the movie Mummy please?
Not now, so run along and play
I'm tidying your bedroom
But we will go soon

Years went by, day by day
Jobs all seemed to get in the way
At last I did get them done
And then thought wouldn't it be great to have some fun?

Yes dear, let's go swimming today
Not now Mum, I'm going out with Faye
Oh please dear, let's go to the swings
Really Mum, I'm too old for those things!
Of course dear, let's go to a movie then
Not now Mum, I'm already going . . . with Ben.

Carey Sellwood

THE EMPTY HOUSE

The old house has been battered by wind and rain:
All day its empty rooms have echoed to the thunder's roll:
But now as darkness falls there is a lull,
A faint light lingers on the horizon.

She turns the heavy key in the rusted lock
And enters this ancient home of her ancestors.
She has come halfway across the world
To see this unexpected inheritance,
Peopled, it seems, by ghosts of long dead antecedents.

Old timbers creak and groan, mice scuttle rapidly away,
As she shines her torch around these empty rooms,
Full of deep shadows, scent of mould, decay.
Her nerves are stretched, she jumps at every sound,
Fearing to see some ghostly apparition,
Some spirit from the shrouded past.
And then -
She sees it -
Crawling slowly across the windowpane,
Partly concealed by curtaining cobwebs,
Inching its way slowly, oh so slowly,
Stealthily reaching up towards the crack,
The splintered glass that lets in eddying draughts.
Her nervous fingers press the switch,
The torch light vanishes,
She is enveloped in foul darkness.
Desperately she seeks to reinstate the light.
At last, the beam shines out
Upon a silver trail across the glass.
Naught else -
The slothful snail has gone.

Roma Davies

GILL

I know a young lady called Gill;
Though turned fifty, she's not over the hill.
What skill on a scooter -
No need for a hooter -
As long as she stays standing still.

David Varley

BREAKFAST SPELL

Rest awhile in cool clear waters
Summon fires from Saturn's daughters
When the bubbles form and rise
In headlong torrent to the skies
Measure must begin of sun's demise
Mark one in twenty parts of the hour
Then dowse the heat
Lest best intentions sour
Carry the orb in majesty to its seat
Ceremony now dictates
A last act to make the play complete
And reveal what the shell encapsulates
One swift cut to tailor the cap
Doff and delve to delights inside
With a finger of bread to open the trap
Yielding white flesh opens wide
Giving forth a golden treasure
Contemplate, then gently season
Body and mind lost in pleasure
Palette's sensors lose their reason
.. This simple method and its alchemy
Creates that illusive perfect soft boiled egg
For you and me . . .

Norman Elsdon

ON MY OWN

I went for a walk tonight and I went all alone,
I walked and walked for miles and miles till my feet hurt to the bone.
I never stopped nor rested, I just walked and walked some more,
No time to stop and rest my legs, though they were aching sore.
I just kept looking straight ahead as I stepped right out,
I felt quite strange and lonely with not a soul about.
But still I kept on walking in the blackness of the night,
The shadowy figures scaring me as they kept coming into sight.
I kept on looking straight ahead, not looking left nor right,
My breathing getting deeper, my chest now feeling tight.
A long, dark road lay ahead of me, where on earth was I heading for
on this blackened night?
A storm arose quite sudden, panic take hold,
I was getting soaked to the skin and feeling very cold.
I just kept on walking and saw someone in my sight,
A shape of tall black darkness passed by me on the right.
I turned around to say hello but no one was in sight.
I ran and ran and did not stop till I couldn't run no more,
My heart was pounding rapidly, my limbs were aching sore.
But still I kept on walking in the darkness of the night,
Till suddenly in front of me was a glimmer of light.
I staggered slowly until I came upon a house
and gladly knocked on the door,
I heard a scream and turned around and the rain began to pour.
I turned around to knock again and froze to see it gone,
I huddled up to the nearest tree too scared to carry on.
I never was so terrified when I heard another scream,
I then awoke just petrified to find it all a dream.

Tina Kelly

A FAIRY STORY

Once upon a time and long ago
In a forest glade I know
Two statues stood (of marbled stone)
Unadorned and all alone
Forms of Adonis and Aphrodite
Carved as if by someone mighty
400 years they'd stood in glory
And this gives credence to my story -
As moonlight bathed the matchless pair
A fairy (floating on the air)
Offered to grant their dearest pleasure
For giving delight in so much measure
'Let us become human' was their request
'For 24 hours, now that we're blest'
'Granted' said the fairy, 'enjoy the fun
Your wish will come true in the morning sun'
And sure enough as that golden globe rose
They both were freed from their sculptured pose
And went into the bushes that grew nearby -
Then there was heard a gasp and a sigh
A squeal and a shout of 'Yes, yes! I agree
It was just the delight that we thought it would be -
Can we do it again?' said the voice 'in a bit?'
'Yes!' the reply 'but then
You hold the pigeon whilst I pooh on it!'

Derek Dodds

TRICK OR TREAT

Just hold my hand, don't be afraid,
the dark can't hurt, it's simply made
by lack of light, our torch will show,
there's nothing to fear . . . not here, oh no!

It's just a face, don't be afraid,
a hollowed out pumpkin simply made
with nose and mouth, and teeth, and eyes,
lit by a candle, hidden inside.

It's only a toy, a video game
no one is hurt, just start again.
Now try to shoot them, catch them off guard,
get your gun, turn quicker . . . yes, it is hard.

What's the problem? Why did you cry?
It's a film, a story . . . did somebody die?
It hasn't happened, it's an actor . . . see?
It isn't real like you and me.

You can't believe what you see on TV,
it could all be virtual reality!
Adventures in space, or beyond the tomb,
directed and broadcast to your own front room.

A child appeared at my door today,
'trick or treat' was all he'd say.
So I gave him a coin and a toffee, no more,
and wondered what trick he had in store.

I heard on the news, of a suicidal raid
by ruthless people who cruelly played
on the trust of a people, whose freedom's renowned,
who couldn't believe it, when the towers fell down.

Alex Marsh

A RUDE AWAKENING

JEB the jolly sailor
Fell hard for pretty Vi;
She promised she'd be faithful,
'I'll love you 'til I die.'
They wed; alas, disaster!
On honeymoon in Skye,
He spied 'I love you Arthur'
Tattooed upon her thigh.

Corinne Lovell

THE CAT WITH NO TAIL

There's a tale to regale
Of a cat with no tail
Don't expect any thanks
From this cat called a Manx
Isle of Man they come from
Could be called Major Tom
Had they all been male
But girls could get crabby
Common sense should prevail
So called Major Tabby

Did they have tails before
They were caught in the door?
Were their tails just cut off
Used as stoles for a toff
Or perhaps used as slippers
Whilst dining on kippers
More questions than answers
At the end of these stanzas
'You were destined to fail'
Miaows the cat with no tail
'And what you've never had
You've surely never missed
For if you have no tail
There is nothing to twist'

John Smurthwaite

ONLY TIME WILL TELL

You never read the signals or even see the signs
You just seemed to lose yourself in the realms in time
On more than one occasion, I redeemed the situation
Alas it was a waste, you weren't paying attention

Life goes on from day to day, week in week out
Watching from a distance with an element of doubt
Always left wondering why, what could the next move be
Let nature takes its course and just wait and see

Years pass by, fate or luck throw you back together again
Will it be rain and sunshine, or misery and pain
However a little spark has always remained
And given time sparks can turn into flames

Learning about one another - starting all over again
Rekindle the fire - don't put out the flame
It's gonna take time to sort things out, but then I'll have to wait
Time I have in abundance, don't be a day too late

Don't worry about the gossip - what other people think and say
You only come here once, sometimes a price you have to pay
It'll be worth it in the long run just you wait and see
I can't wait to see people's faces when they realise it's me

Leigh Smart

THE MYSTERY

One dark, damp, winter's night
As I lay in my bed
Fast asleep, dreaming
Dreamt that I was dead.
Suddenly a dreadful noise
Woke me from my sleep,
I heard voices and music
That came from the deep,
Of my mind, at first I thought
Still in a sleepy daze,
Sat bolt up in my bed
My eyes around did gaze,
Decided I, must be brave
Lamp help in my hands,
Was it ghosts or burglars?
I walked with shaking hand,
Through the long, dark corridor
Into the dining room,
Expected to be pounced upon
Nothing in the gloom,
My radio was playing
Blasting in my ears,
I must admit it scared me
Adding to my fears,
Chills ran up and down my spine,
Whatever could it be?
The timer on my radio
What a silly me.

J Naylor

WHAT COULD BE

Wholesome that's beside the point,
It's just a nice, big, juicy joint,
I know I'm hungry and on a diet,
But if I don't eat soon, I'd just as cry it,
It's not that much I want to take,
And not as if I've asked for cake,
Beef or bread, nice slice of toast,
Soon I'll look like someone's ghost,
Not to scare, but thin and lean,
People will say you're truly mean,
Let your wife eat now, for all our sake,
Don't want her to call bedtime
And have us awake,
A crumb can I have, a biscuit or two,
They're mean in our house, some even got flu,
You're truly bedraggled, is what people say,
It's terrible your husband won't go out of his way,
To see if you're well fed, clothed and shorn,
Nice to look at each and every morn,
You say it's high time your hunger enjoy,
A big slice of bacon, or sausage, deploy,
I reach out, I'm hungry, what those people gave nice,
Although with crumbs we'd soon have the mice
As my right hand goes out for
That big piece of cake,
I feel tug, on my shoulder, hey mum, please awake,
You're having a dream,
Hey mum, wake up please.

Hugh Campbell

THE SNAKE AND THE BUTTERFLY

The snake.
Slithered and writhed.
It slid over sand and shale.
Over rocks and fallen trees
It slunk, silently,
Between blades of grass.
Eyes never wavering,
Fixed permanently,
On the butterfly,
Which blithely fed,
On the nectar of an orchid.
The snake head stopped.
Inches from the ephemera
The rest of its body
Continued to move until,
Curled up beneath itself,
It poised tensed and taut,
Eyes unmoving.
Tongue flickering:
The butterfly finished,
Siphoning the nectar.
Stroked its tube.
Scraped a little pollen,
Onto and from the orchid.
Its body flexed down,
Its six legs pushed.
Its wings swept.
It lifted from the flower.
The snake struck.

Missed!
Happy me!
Happy butterfly!

Sad snake.

Harry Lyons

WHILE GRANDMOTHER WAITED
(A story remembered from my grandmother's life)

My grandmother's sister Evelyn, asked her if,
She would go to a séance with her one day,
But grandmother, had taught Sunday school in church,
And remembered what the bible had to say.
Do not meddle with the spirits of the dead,
But Eleanor, I need someone to accompany me there, she said,
My grandmother was not scared, or filled with dread,
And grandmother told Evelyn that she would go,
I will sit outside the room, instead.
After a while travelling to this place,
Where things are told from souls displaced,
Evelyn said, Eleanor don't you want your future told?
Grandmother said, if my future's planned then no I don't.
As grandmother waited in the room outside,
In moving air the candles flickered,
And in a sudden chill she swiftly shivered,
Grandmother felt a sudden ice push through her,
Her skin dampened and chilled, this really threw her,
This happened for a second and third time,
While she waited there, in the room alone,
She felt these wakened souls walk through, into the other room.
My grandmother was told when Evelyn came back,
There were three ghosts in the room doing mischief, freed,
Yes said Grandmother, there were three spirits,
They went into your room, but they came through Me.

Susan Carole Roberts

STRANGE BIRDS

All afternoon the strange birds fly
Against the blue vault of the sky,
Hang and hover, dip and glide
Along the wooded mountainside.

With coloured bands, their wings outspread
In gold and yellow, white and red,
Before the wind they gather pace,
They turn about with casual grace.

Then softly, gently, come to land,
And from the roadside where we stand
We see, in watching their descents,
They are young men with parapents!

Evelyn Westwood

RIVALRY

Your sister was a friend to you
When your life was so demanding.
To me she seems so mixed up
And takes some understanding.

She taunts me, she torments me,
Puts temptation in my way.
How can I help but wonder,
I think she wants to play.

This mouth-watering opportunity
Sends shivers down my spine.
Far reaching possibilities
If only she were mine.

This trial and error has got to stop
Before I go berserk.
A sigh of satisfaction
Before someone gets hurt.

The rivalry between you
I see it from afar.
But faith can move a mountain
No matter where you are.

Sometimes I find you very sweet
But you have a heart of stone.
So now I choose your sister
And you are left alone.

Charles B Warcup

ABC

My grandfather was shoeing his horse one day
He'd removed the shoe and trimmed the hoof OK
He needed a special tool which couldn't be found
in order to fetch this, he let the horse foot down

The next second he had been kicked in the head
My poor distraught grandmother in panic said
to the girls 'Quickly, run and fetch the ABC'
when really what she wanted was the TCP

Now when I read that TCP label today
Use this for all insect stings burns and spots they say
but never have they claimed or I've heard it said
TCP is good for a horse kick in the head

Valerie Ovais

THE GROTTO

Do you believe in Christmas and its magic spell -
Do you visit the grotto where gnomes and fairies dwell?
They say it's a time for children, but adults also cherish
The look on children's faces, as their presents they relish.
But, sometimes, hopes are dashed and people have to bear
Disappointments at this time, as I can swear.
I wanted to be a fairy, but they made me a gnome instead,
With bulging eyes and a little red nose and a pointed hat on my head.
I wanted to be a fairy, with wings and a tinsel wand,
But they said the part had to go to an attractive blonde.
They girl they chose had long legs that went right up to her chin,
And worst of all, in my eyes, she was sickeningly thin!
I wanted to be a fairy, to shine on the Christmas tree,
But they said I was too heavy - which was rude, you must agree.
So I have to sit by the grotto pool, with my rod and string and pin,
Waving at all the children and wearing a soppy grin.
But there's a destiny that shapes our ends, as a famous poet said,
Because one day, as it turned out, matters came to a head.
I saw her in a corner, with Prince Charming, having a snog -
So I waved my little rod - and turned him back to a frog!

B Gordon

LIFE'S LIKE THAT

A deck of cards held in my hand
Would suffice to tell the tale
And time's run out - like sifted sand
Now lifted is the veil
I held the game - and it was mine
With no thought for next deal
The king, the queen, the jack, the nine
Fortune too good for real.

'Twas not for me to realise the next play was my last
False mistress chance - I did provoke her
What matters now? All in the past
My next play was the joker!

Jeanette M Tucker

THE PRESENT

A stranger called at a door one day,
    placed in the owner's hand
A small package he said he'd found
On the doorstep, not wishing it to get wet.
Upon reading to whom it was written,
    they declined to receive, explaining,
    it was not meant for them you see.
The message, penned in an unknown hand
    was addressed to -
    'The One Who Blesses With their Eyes'.
Surprised they had refused, thinking it
    some jest;
The stranger looked at them, shook his head
    and with a gentle stare, said
'You have not been looking up at stars.'
The remark startled them.
Giving back the package once again,
    he courteously raised his hat,
    and turning departed in the rain.
At first, hesitating,
    the parcel then was opened, to find
    within
    a perfectly shaped oval stone, golden;
Upon which her name was written.

Janine Vallor

INDIAN MEAL

There was this Indian gentleman,
We wanted to impress,
We met him at the station,
We'd put on evening dress!

We took him to this Indian place,
The very best we knew,
And after some discussion
We chose chicken Vindaloo.

Kashmiri soup for starters,
And Jalebis for sweet,
Rogan Josh and Kofta Balls
And curried lobster meat.

We thought lime and mango pickle
And some hot Tikka Aloo,
Perhaps a Biryani,
And a Papadam or two.

The waiter then approached us
As we start licking out lips.
That's when our Indian gentleman
Ordered - egg and chips!

M Mettam

WHEN A LEAF IS NOT A LEAF

Heavenly hunters ride the skies, when summer fades,
To start their great bloodthirsty raids!
Exploring misty crevices for the Great Bear.
Determined to find his hidden lair!

The victim is discovered and rendered dead!
Healthy green leaves are splashed with red!
Inaudible sound of the Great Bears' bellow!
Fat from the kettle splatters yellow!

The curtain opens on a dramatic scene!
Jack Frost's war on the leaves of green!
Transforming colours of summer with paint pot in hand!
Thinking browns and reds look much more grand!

Cool, crisp nights chase the trail of bright, lighted days!
Autumn's bright hues begin to blaze!
Green pigments cannot survive without saps' life!
Severed stems, as if cut with a knife!

Jack Frost and the Great Bear are not painting the tree!
It decides itself the leaves must be free!
Conserving water is the essential thing,
Or there will be no buds of spring!

Extravaganza of colour, shroud of glory!
The plum-coloured ash starts the story!
Scarlet oak leaf pursues vibrant-brown beech.
Floating down, with the ground in their reach!

My mother said words that I must have mistook.
'Take a leaf from your brother's book!'
But which book and which leaf I haven't a clue!
So, I must leave the choice up to you!

Val Spall

LIFE AFTER PAIN

The pain is stronger now
As it ebbs and flows through me.
The beads of sweat build up
Through every pore on my face.
I can hear my husband's panic
As he urges me to breathe.
I look into a stranger's eyes
And see some kindness there.
Who are all these people,
Standing round me now?
Watching as I suffer,
Can't they watch TV instead?
I grip a hand that's laying in mine,
As the pain intensifies.
It surges through me,
Ouch that hurt!
Why can't it hurry up?
I feel as if my insides
Are trying to get out.
To think I chose all this.
I must have been insane.
I surely won't do this again.
yet I did. But, only because
The bundle they finally laid in my arms
Was my daughter
Warm, soft, dependant, and filled with love.

Trisha Walton

AGE HELPS YOU SEE

Tomorrow is another day that never does arrive,
It gives us hope I have to say, the hope to stay alive.
But what the future holds today, could all be gone, tomorrow.
And every night I hope and pray, that day won't bring me sorrow.
How once my future looked so bright, then changed with just one act.
I thought that I was always right, I'm not and that's a fact.
I cared not of the world around, I only cared for me.
I never saw the gifts abound, the fruits of life there be.
My mam and dad were gentle, gentle to the core
And I just drove them mental, and then I pushed some more.
The words they said I never heard, I passed them off as duff.
I guess that's why I did some bird, and my life turned out tuff.
I've cried myself to sleep at night, by lonely high street doors,
I've interfered in every fight, peacemaker was my cause.
I never feared the strangers, befriending every soul,
I never saw the dangers, until I knew each goal.
But one thing learned, I now can say
Respect is earned, and not all pray.
Nor do they follow rules, or care about your heart
They just see us as fools' they use, and then depart.
I wished to be a soldier; I would have been the best.
But all I got is older; I missed my chance, my quest.
Each person has a different road, not knowing where it ends
And seldom will we share our load, for seldom we find friends.
But in amongst the jaded minds, friends can still be found,
You'll see the light, so bright it blinds, and then my words be sound.
For only two, will truly care, the path of life you choose.
And waste today we must not dare, for tomorrow, we could lose.
The souls that gave us life, who aid us in this world.
They've seen us through the pains and strife, whilst words of hate
we hurled.
I hope tomorrow brings you hope, and you soon see the light.
'Cause they'll be there to help you cope, their love is true and right.
My mam and dad are ageing fast, forever, growing weak
I know not which day will be last, their love I yearn, I seek.

It's only since my dad, took me to one side
And said, 'Now listen lad, you fill my heart with pride.'
That I began to understand, the pains I'd put him through.
I was the fool, as he did brand, the words he said were true.
He saw my path of choosing; he begged I shouldn't take it
And he knew I'd be losing, and said I'd never make it.
The words he spoke, turned out so true
He said 'Young bloke the fall's for you.'
For path he said I'd find, to help me on my way.
Was helping ease a saddened mind, at least one everyday?
Well help I try to do, hope I try to give,
And these words now for you, I hope will help you live.
You control the outcome, the way your life will be
But you must heed your dad and mum, 'cause best for you they see.
If I had heard the worlds he said, twenty years ago,
My path may not have wrecked my head, and my talent
the world would know.

Geoffrey Woodhead

MY FIRST-BORN

I look on him so many times
During the day and night -
Just to make sure all is well
And everything's alright.
So small, and yet so perfect,
How did I create such wonder?
So soft to my gentle touch
Like silk or velvet under
My fingers. Six weeks ago
He was not here.
Endlessly I awaited his birth
In such anxiety and fear.
I had not realised how long
I would have to endure
The suspense. Was I too old, inexperienced
To raise this hope for the future?
It did not help that
He was over two weeks late.
Had I miscalculated
The time. Mistaken the date?
Then six weeks ago he appeared
So tiny and dependant upon me.
I gave him such loving care -
This my first home-grown Sweet Pea.

Joyce Hockley

THE NEW YEAR

Christmas is over, and thank God for that!
The meals prepared, eaten and supped,
Gone are the blues from a hangover before,
Mopping the blood, sweat and tears, from the floor!

Now the New Year, equally a bore,
With cold roast chicken, only the cat wants more!
The mistletoe curling, long past its day,
Leaving all who enter, in a daze.

Feeling limp, the hour is here,
For those who wish to celebrate the New Year,
Listening in, for the bells to toll,
As others decide to take a stroll.

Under the fountain, both cold and wet,
The atmosphere riddled with suspense and fear,
As police control the crowds that have formed,
Occasionally, it comes to a family who mourn.

After midnight, they all disperse
With empty bottles, they are the worst,
They spoil the celebration that innocent people want,
As the tension rises with the volume of their chant!

The morning after, just look at the floor,
With wasted peanuts, mince pies, and more,
Often with a headache with the anticlimax to show,
Just how the season is left, I really don't know!

On the twelfth night, the cards come down,
Often with a rain of dust, as we frown,
Thank God for that, we all sigh with relief,
No more of that, for 353 days, good grief!

Rosemary E Pearson

MISS TWENTY

It's been a long time since I've known you and I'm going to
                                        miss you so
The future's so uncertain I don't know where to go
We've lived through good and bad times, you've always been
                                        by my side
But now you're going from me I've nowhere left to hide.

Goodbye Miss Twenty I'm going to miss you so
The curtains coming down on us it's the end of our show
Goodbye to Miss Twenty and the tapestry you've sown
I'm falling for a new woman the likes I've never known.

I'm going to miss your ways but, then again, I'm not
When our love was running smoothly it's the bad times I forgot
You were such a volatile woman, a different side I saw every day
Because I never fully understood you I'm somehow glad
                                        you're going away.

All the pain you gave me the sorrow and the tears
The heartache and the sadness I've known throughout the years
You gave from me and you took from me, you let me have my day
But it was always your final will that won in every way;
You let me think I was in control when really I was not
You composed each and every chapter and fired all the shots.

So goodbye Miss Twenty I'm really leaving you this time
But the future's so uncertain as I prepare to cross the line
I know that I will miss you, your familiar little ways
As I live my life without you through all my future days,
Let's just say it was inevitable and I hope things turn out fine
Goodbye to Miss Twenty your century's run out of time.

Gareth Harvey

THAT KISS

Thank you for that kiss
Which you gave to me.
It left me speechless.

On the true surface
I'm so full of glee.
Thank you for that kiss.

I was left helpless,
Being blind to see.
It left me speechless.

There was no shyness
Which you may agree.
Thank you for that kiss.

Now I've such fondness
I can guarantee
It left me speechless.

With it there's richness
Which can never be.
Thank you for that kiss;
It left me speechless.

Edward Ward

THE VILLAGE PUB
THE CARPENTER AND THE UNICORN

In all villages there has been
A church, a school, a village green,
A local pub, and a shop
A local hall for the village hop,
In Great Rollright, a pub well worn
It was always called, The Unicorn,
Many generations enjoyed the beer
A game of Aunt Sally, at the rear.

A game of dominoes and darts
And a friendly game of cards,
All went well, until one landlord came
Soon things would not be the same,
One Monday morning dark and grey
In January, a deep snow lay,
A carpenter and a bailiff came
Rollright was never to be the same.

The landlord not expecting them to come
Had lit the fire, to warm him some,
The bailiff said, the landlord had to go
And turned him out into the snow,
Then for the carpenter to do his bit
A brand new set of locks to fit,
As the snow lay all around
They had made not a sound.

So when that evening came along
The locals, they did carry on,
To find The Unicorn had no light
And never again to open at night,
So the locals, were so very sad
They were in fact, hopping mad,
No clues had been left around
As the snow lay on the ground.

Not a word from the landlord, of his plight
Nor from the carpenter, that drank last night,
For as the village woke that morn
The pair of them had struck at dawn,
So now you see the stories out
The bailiff, he was very stout,
Now it is all plain to see
That little carpenter was me.

Martin J Harvey

YOU'RE THE CAT'S WHISKERS

My girlfriend had just left me
So I was feeling sad and lonely
When suddenly you flitted into the room
Like a model on the catwalk
But I could see you were no phoney
And the left side of my chest just went boom

There was no pause or hesitation
You looked so lovely in your fur coat
Move into my flat this afternoon
Leave that man in Berkeley Mews
With his mistress up in Eastcote
Stay with me or life will be a mournful tune

I've heard those dreadful rumours
Of your nights out on the tiles
How you're affected by the phases of the moon
But it's only half expected
With those charming feminine wiles
Promise Tiddles that you'll come and live here soon

Stuart Delvin

THE STRANGEST DAY

When I went to school one day,
There were no children out to play,
There were no friends for gossip to tell,
They didn't sound the morning bell.
And when I went into the class,
There were no tests for me to pass,
The dinner hall was also bare,
Even the headmaster wasn't there
I didn't know quite what to do,
So there I stood in quite a stew.
Then I remembered telling my friend
I'll meet you tomorrow,
It's the weekend.

Judith Mason

BACK OF THE CHURCH

The wedding
Nudged by his young son at the wedding, John was asked how high
can an eagle fly and how deep does a mole dig to make its home
Awakening his senses he bowed to the questions demanding,
how and why
John's mind had been enticed to roam for though the choir sang,
it wasn't heard
Only to be greeted by a deathly silence, quieter than a winter's
setting sun
Bells rang when they arrived at the country church, and birds sang
from high in the sycamore trees
Only moments before the bride and groom had been down on their
knees praying and taking their vows
At the back of the church were two mice, who up till now had
been dreaming of scraps from left-over dinners as the wedding
gathering listened to tales about wise men and out and out sinners
No, this wasn't a day for nervous beginners
The bride sure looked pretty in her white wedding gown, as did the
three bridesmaids and her mama too
Meanwhile, the two mice danced a gig
Skipping around a knotted ash twig like it was a mousetrap with
neither wanting to die
One threw up his top hat, did a pirouette and scurried off and hid
The other, bold as brass, and of low class with taps on his feet
went on to perform a slick routine he had learnt on the street
A copy of the Sporting Life tucked in his back pocket he had his eye on
the bride's gold locket as he leaped up high
Spun twice, and on dropping to the floor he rolled over head over heels
Damn it, if that wasn't great, and by far the slickest thing the boys
ever did
Then . . . on running outside he jumped up, hugging and kissing the
ugliest of pigs on his way
Tears of joy and laughter flooding out from the church
To the extent that five were drowned, two of which have never
been found

Mickey the jester and Joy the clown
The vicar known for being a bit of wag and dressing in drag couldn't
take any more
Feeling weak at the knees he let out a mighty sneeze to send
the groom's hat spinning through the air
Landing perfectly, on the bemused church cat who had been working
off some excess fat
Meanwhile, crazy Alice was running around, telling everyone
that listened that she was to be married next
The vicar getting to read an extra special text
By he way if you are reading this and would like to book this amazing
duo then phone the office, and ask for Sid
The cost being a hundred quid

Maurice Hope

LOVE KNOWS NO BARRIER

I hear her footsteps down the hall,
My heart begins to beat a pace,
What a precious gift for me,
To look upon her smiling face.

She comes to me, I take her hand,
Her fragrance takes my breath away,
And once again I'm at a loss,
I cannot find the words to say.

To tell her what she means to me,
Would take the poet's words, not mine,
And yet I know she understands,
Our love fulfils God's great design.

She does not need to say a word,
I know her thought, her every mood,
Just like me, she would reveal,
Her heart's desire, if e'er she could.

I never cease to be amazed,
That love was meant for such as we,
But no one has a greater need,
For she can't speak and I can't see.

Michael McKenna

MODEL REQUIREMENT

Interview -
Shaky knees.
Could be you -
'Come in, please.'

Legs so slim -
Little bust.
Extra thin -
Now a 'must'.

Elfin hair,
Soft and fine.
Tinted fair -
Modern line.

Eyebrows right -
Lashes curled.
Eyes so bright,
Eyelids 'pearled'.

Cheeks like silk -
Gentle blush.
Moisture milk,
Camel brush.

Lips a dream -
Subtle gloss.
Teeth that gleam -
Dental floss.

Lovely smile -
May we start?
Wait awhile -
Can't take part!

Thought you knew! You were told.
Twenty-two! Far too old!

Pat Watson

SPOOKS YOU SIR!

Dave aged twenty bought a suit
To his surprise he found it haunted
He wore it to an interview
Which he so badly wanted

Every time he pulled the jacket on
He felt a shiver down his spine
He thought nothing of it
Because this wasn't the first time

When he took his jacket off at night
It moved by itself
Ghostly footsteps were heard outside Dave's door
When all of a sudden his jacket fell to the floor

All I wanted was a good-looking suit
Instead I got a haunted one
It didn't cost much
A really neat sum

I hired a preacher to tell what was wrong
He told me my suit was cursed
After praying and laying on hands
No more was the suit cursed

Dave's happy wearing his suit
But most of his friends
Think it was all a big hoot

They nicknamed him Casper
My friends thought it was funny
But little did they know
The suit was well worth its money.

Lisa Brown (15)

THE AWAKENING

Listen, I hear space between any sound
Perfect moments, silence all around
I hold, smell and touch, this thin slice of time
Empty, nothing - everything, and all mine
For in such a short while it will invert
A snapping, snarling noise my ears will hurt
Like a cat scratching, hissing, defending her young
A foul growling, scowling, howling from one
With teeth that spit, gnashing to and fro
An eagle holding its lair from predatory foe
Or a cobra waiting to jump, biting the hand from which it feeds
No point protesting, no kindness, no point in pleads
Here is a wild animal released from a trap, the rage
How dare I, yes me, how dare I rattle her cage?
But not yet, for now all is still
Quiet, calm, so tranquil just until
I advance and position the tea in her breakfast cup
'Morning Darling Daughter - it's time to wake up.'

J Barry

BOY IN THE RED CAP

Huffing on the sidewalk
On a hot, sunny day,
Got to the traffic lights,
Hindering my way.

The red had turned to amber
Just as I reached the road,
I'd done a hasty stop
And scattered all my load.

The two-seater coupé
Then caught my eye,
As he revved up his engine,
To swiftly pass me by.

But in that flash second,
To acknowledge my mishap,
He sent forth his smile to me,
And briefly touched his cap.

His cap, it was red,
And jauntily tilted,
On his blond, curly hair,
My annoyance just wilted.

For his blue eyes laughed,
And sparkled sunshine,
And for a brief second,
I wished he was mine.

With his open top coupé,
And his red cap and all,
But I wasn't his Cinderella,
To take to the Ball.

For that boy in the auto,
Who smiled across at me,
Was, I suppose, about twenty
And I was sixty-three!

Aleene Hatchard

DESERT LAND

You're in a desert,
The sun is blazing,
A burning ball of gas,
A ball hovering in the sky,

It burns down onto you,
Sizzling your skin,
Colouring everything,
Rosy red.

Grains of sand,
No path to follow,
No grains of grass,
No twigs from fallen trees,

Your thirst is dry,
Your lips are cracked,
Your eyes are weak,
Your body aches,

For the need,
Of water to moist your lips,
To trickle down your throat,
To bang down on your skin,

To cool down your burning skin.

R Hanson

TRACEY'S BED

Tracey has shown her bed
Unmade
No worry she cannot now
Lie on it

Tracey has feathered her nest
Saatchi has seen to that
No need
To take heed
Of the future

He has the bed
And she has the cash
His to lie on
And hers to rely on.

Joseph Smedley

THE CONTEMPLATIVE CAT

The contemplative cat
comes into Meeting
silently, stealthily,
seeking his place -
as member of the Assembly,
suddenly energetic,
he leaps up
to his chosen bench:
rustles the papers
until observing a cushion nearby -
he moves cautiously along
and there he curls up
with economy of effort
and innate grace,
He observes the silence
faithfully, better perhaps
than we humans!
But, who knows what he made
of the message of light?
Cats are nocturnal creatures!

Muriel E Critoph

THE TIN PLATE

He was old and gnarled like an old oak tree
He lived with his daughter and her little girl
He was feeble and shaky and dropped things at will
If the truth be told he was far from well
His daughter was always ranting and raving and giving him hell
Of temper short and horrid with it
She was a bit of a tyrant and not nice at all
Which did not help his cause very much
He kept on breaking things, poor old soul
Even his daughter's prized sugar bowl
Then one day at the market she spotted a solution
To the main problem which was dinner time
It was a tin dinner plate
She came home in triumph, 'He won't break this,' she declared
His little granddaughter looked on in dismay
As she planked down the plate on a metal tray
His dinner was even noisier than before
But still he kept dropping things on the floor
As was inevitable, things came to a head
One day the old man was found to be dead
After all the crocodile tears and all the fuss
She gathered up his stuff to put out in the bin
Including his tin plate amongst other things
Later that day she heard a rumble outside
Looking out she saw her wee girl plundering the bin
'What are you looking for?' she said to her
'The tin plate,' was the reply
'It's only rubbish now,' said her mum
'No,' said the daughter, I'm saving it
Because some day I may need it for you.'

James Rodger

THE LANDING OF THE ROMANS

The galley sails towards this strange land,
An eerie silence fills the air.
The mists engulf us,
The black murky water surrounds the boat.
Gloomy sky hanging angrily over us.
Nothing about this land reminds us of home,
Where the warm sun is always shining.
None of it is here in this desolate place.
We huddle together in uneasy groups,
Sharing rumours about the savage people who
                              inhabit this damp island.
A blue daubed figure darts out from behind a tree,
The handles of our swords sweat as we grip them tightly.
Suddenly,
An unearthly cry fills our heads with fear.
We huddle closer together,
Another cry rings out, breaking the short silence.
It is as if the forest has erupted.
Loud war cries ring out over the shallows,
Reaching our galley like a forceful blow.
Neighing of frightened horses join the roar,
We knew it was war.
With a cry of our own,
We leap into the swirling water,
Our swords and shields gripped tightly,
As we prepare to fight for our Empire.

Craig Lye (9)

THE ATTACK

With lion-like tread he stalks his prey.
Behind a bush he hides; waits to attack,
Knowing she will come his way:
Then he'll leap upon her back.

Heedless, she runs across the field;
Across the so-familiar grass:
Careless of what a bush may shield,
A little bush which she must pass.

Esmé sees the lurking cat.
She leaps first upon his back.
It was not meant to be like that,
That she, herself, should first attack.

Catsby swears and runs away.
He'll try again some other time.
Two friends, a cat and dog at play,
The happy subject of my rhyme.

Frances Joan Tucker

WILD THINGS

There are lions in our garden
But not the ferocious kind
In fact they are very docile
But to my mind they are a bind

They stand there very proudly
Their golden heads in the air
I have tried to make them go away
They drive me to despair

I shall have to take drastic action
And dig very deep, I fear
But I know whatever I do
The dandelions will be back next year.

Olive Homer

UNMET IN LOVE

Unmet in love: I am alone:
Lianne is a beautiful
Twenty-seven year old sight,
As I think of her, in my mind,
My heart, my soul, fifty-five:
I see two magpies sitting
In the November rain,
Tails twitching, on a
Railway roof
Met in love:
Unmet in love: I am alone:

Unmet in love: I am alone:
Thinking of wonderful, Lianne:
So much is changing in my
Fifty-five year old short life:
Yet I am standing perfectly
Still; as, Lianne is leaving
To walk this world, Australia,
South America, so beautiful,
So tragic, this planet Earth:
Unmet in love: I am alone:

Unmet in love: I am alone:
Met in love, two blackbirds
Wing now the evening, November,
Rain, met in love their feathers
Touching in mid-air:
Unmet in love: I am alone.

Edmund Saint George Mooney

THE HAUNTED WOOD

If you should go into the dark woods
Tonight . . . Beware! Beware!
Ghosts and spectres from brotherhoods
And chill the midnight air.

The screaming wind is roaring fast,
And hark! An old church bell,
Chiming, blaring like terror aghast,
Roaming wild o'er peak and fell.

The birds are quiet, their songs have died,
Silent so it seems for evermore,
'Cept for a raven's cry, echoing far and wide,
Piercing the ears of the valley's floor.

Bristly hedgehogs curl-up into a ball,
Retreating to their dank, earthen lair,
Shunning with badgers their food withall,
Deathly fearful of the forest's glare.

Ghostly phantoms faint and flicker
In and out of the full moon's glow,
And up in front - an elfish critter
Precedes the path of death and woe.

And hark! The death knell sounds its ken
As strange, lurid shapes, nigh surround,
With interludes sounding again and again,
Haunting the pathways of this cursed ground.

Heys Stuart Wolfenden

LE MONDE ON A MONDAY

Although I may add a special ending,
I will seldom do it with a twist.
I am not one for switch blades
Or deceitful ways like this.

The very antithesis of boredom
Is this twist within the tail . . .
As with the deadly sting of scorpions
Who will sceptically derail.

I admired the way that Alfred Hitchcock
Always let you know the score
As he played with your suspense sense
Without ever being a bore.

Amongst those who tried to lie and cheat
I reluctantly cite A Christie,
For she did more than shield the truth
Or come on a little 'misty'.

Not, then, just mistiness, but foggy,
With blind blanket deception.
She trusted one would not recall
Where one had had one's misconception.

My real literary hero,
The sanguine self personified.
Perfection fulfilled with perfect ease.
P G Wodehouse never lied.

His tales of intricate intrigue
Reached impossibly delightful endings.
I claim no one in English literature
Has surpassed the Wodehouse rendings.

For *my* twist I'll add a twist of *Le Mon de*,
The blond world is more fun and funds will get more blondes.

Robert John Moore

THE LANDLADY

There she stood straight and grim
Buxom with a double chin,
Arms firmly folded across her chest
Landlady of 'The Seaview West'

'I see you managed to find the way
There are some rules you must obey
No eating or cooking in the rooms
No loud radios playing tunes.
No visitors allowed at night
Especially men, it's just not right..

I looked at Joe, he looked at me
'I hope we're not too late for tea!'
'Tea!' She bellowed loud and clear
'We don't serve tea, not never here.
Bed and breakfast, we provide
Other meals you get outside.

Now come on in and sign the book.'
She said, giving Joe a funny look.
'I'm sure that you will like it here
Some folk come back every year.'

Joe muttered underneath his breath
'I bet it's cos they're scared to death
That if they didn't, she'd swear and curse
Though I can't think of anything worse
Than spending two whole weeks right here
At Seaview West on Wigan Pier!

J M Gallen

MY BEST FRIEND
(To Ch. Almanza Firecracker - Crackers to her friends!)

Tonight my best friend died.
Such a loving, trusting, kindly soul. Never one to give a
nasty answer to any reproof no matter how undeserved.
Always so thrilled to see me at any time of the day or night,
always full of comfort and sympathy when I was ill or when
something was wrong, asking so little in return - I shall
never be able to fill the gap her going leaves in my heart
and my life.

A routine walk was an adventure when she accompanied me,
she had such a zest for living, such a loving interest in everyone
we met. Her friends were numerous, one had only to meet her
once to fall under her spell. It is true that the very odd occasion
she would sulk at what she thought was a slight but she soon
forgave and was her sunny self again.

I was with her to the very end and my presence seemed to
comfort and support her. The 'powers that be' were very good
about letting me stay. Now I am home again and already I miss her.
There is no tombstone for my friend, the vet disposed of her
remains for me, but her memory will live with me forever.

Peg Allen

THE MAGICAL PLACE BEHIND THE DOOR

Wooden doors sat at the end of the hall,
They were opened wide.
Light shone and reflected off the floor,
Did I dare to go inside!
I crept up to the entrance
To get a closer look.
I gazed around in wonder,
It was like something from a book.
At one end of the room sat riches
Of gold and long lost treasure.
Looking the other way I saw
A dragon, impossible to measure.
His head the size of a small cart,
His scales of a deep gold.
His body stretched back for metres,
Into the dark and cold.
His wings were folded across his back,
Their tips touching the ground.
Two pointed ears sat upon his head,
Between them silver was found.
His fangs were a gleaming white,
As long as a person's arm.
His tongue flickered out in a menacing way,
And I forced myself to be calm.
I backed slowly towards the door,
A look of terror upon my face.
And as I left the room I realised,
It was a truly magical place.

Samantha Gildart (13)

WIN OR LOSE - PART TWO

From an early age success is praised
Great store is set upon it
Failure alas is frowned upon
Yet somehow we all know it.

Citizen Kane, Sweet Smell of Success
Great films explore their facets
Success brings power which can corrupt
While failure hurts and scorns our assets.

Favourites do not always win
Outsiders defy the odds
The outcome often hangs on luck
Or favours from the gods.

Imposters both, so Kipling wrote
To meet with steely nerve
Only tenacity of purpose
Gives us rewards that we deserve.

J C Bruford

THE DIAMOND RING

Waver the flame 'pon the candlestick,
dotting the wax on the flagstone flick,
Embers glow in the mouth of the hearth
from out the darkness and evil laugh.
Bedrooms for the guests prepare, the
Inn is filled with Christmas fare.
The publicans, their son awaits, with
game pie and rich raisin cake.
Expectant since the icy dawn, alert
for sound of hoof and horn.
Inside the Mail Coach, joyful ride,
the beautiful girl to be his bride.
No place beside his dearest love,
compelled to sit on top, above.
From out his coat, with pride he brings,
displays a sparkling diamond ring.
Drinking brandy to keep warm, hopes
to reach Bodmin by the dawn.
Better for him in his pocket stayed,
safe from preying eyes it laid.
A charming fellow he thought he knew,
fought for the ring and stabbed him through.
With little hope they carried him, white
and bleeding to the Inn.
Repeat each Christmas this dreadful scene,
gone the joy which might have been.
Cries the poor girl for her love, stain the
flagstone with his blood.
Death, a diamond, life disband,
the girl a phantom, holds his hand.

A E Doney

THE ANGEL OF THEIR DREAM

Their dream was born in childhood
Before wedlock joined their hearts
A dream that lived within their souls
That only death could ever part
They had dreamt an American pilgrimage
A country strewn with gold
A world of fate and opportunity
Where the miracles of life unfold
They had heard the pilgrim's stories
And their excitement grew within
They were to see their life's ambition
Grow to reality from a whim.

They pictured the black hills of Dakota
'Neath a bold and friendly sky
Imagined the mighty Mississippi roll
Passed their blessed and pleasured eyes
They felt the warmth of California
Perceived the awe of Niagara Falls
Their minds accosted the old Grand Canyon
And pined for the New England fall
Thus America became their icon
They were to swop the old for new
And they cradled that moment of happiness
Where every fairytale comes true.

They boarded the pride of Cunard
Like a pretentious king and queen
Thus they saw the proud *Titanic*
As the angel of their dream.

David Bridgewater

REUNION

'How nice to see you Rosalind,
It must be forty years
Since we parted in that cloakroom
In a flood of angry tears.'

'And all because of Alastair,
That gawky bag of bones:
You said I'd pinched him from you
In the last but one Paul Jones.'

'We were a pair of silly girls
To fall in love with him:'
'So arrogant,'
'So ignorant.'
'So cocksure,'
'And so dim!'

'Well, let's forget our foolish past
And have a nice long chat:
And let me tell you Rosalind
How much I like your hat.'

'Oh thank you dear, I put it on
Because its turned much colder:
And Anne, you're simply wonderful.
You don't look one day older.'

'I've made the tea,
There's buttered toast:
Do try my home-made paste.'
'Oh thank you dear, delicious -
But what a funny taste!
I think there must be something wrong,
I feel a little queer.'

'Oh no, there's nothing wrong at all . . .
It's cyanide, my dear.'

E R Low

MY DOG

I love my dog, I love my dog,
Though he weighs nearly fifteen stone,
He's buried me in the garden,
He thinks that I'm a bone.

It's not this that's upset me,
He has done this once before,
It's the fact that he's gone and left me,
And run off with that bitch next door.

J A Jenkins

THE EXILE'S ERROR

He'd been away long years in foreign countries,
  Yes, many many miles his feet had roamed,
But now at last, his wandering days were over,
  He was heading back to sights and sounds of home.

He hadn't even sent a welcome letter
  Or kept in touch at all, all down the years,
Indeed, his family thought he'd died and left them
  And many were the sighs and bitter tears.

But there dawned the day when hopes again were kindled
  For he wrote at last to say he'd see them soon,
He'd be home, he wrote, just as the summer started
  For his ship was sailing on the first of June.

Came the great day and the family gathered, waiting
  To see the wanderer come back at last,
Though hair was whiter and the faces wrinkled
  The smiles were just as bright as in the past.

He strode the path and through the well-known doorway
  And they crowded round and chorused loud 'Hurrah!'
He hugged a white-haired woman saying 'Hello Granny'
  Said she, recoiling 'I'm not yer granny - I'm yer *Ma!*'

Betty McIlroy

DREADFUL PARENTS

We were dreadful parents,
Our boys will tell you that.
We wouldn't let them stay out late,
Or ever answer back.
They couldn't swear, use drugs or drink;
We didn't think it good.
We laid down rules, made them obey,
I'm sure they wanted blood.
Nosy too, we always pried
Into their private lives.
What did they do? Where did they go?
Right 'til they got wives.
We even made them work, you know!
Gave chores to each young man,
And did they mind? I'm sure they did;
And much revenge did plan.
We didn't let them rule the roost;
Our lives around them spin.
We were there, a mum and dad,
'Twas they who fitted in.
Bet they were quick to leave the nest
I almost hear you say:
Couldn't wait to leave, escape,
Get married, run away!
Well no! I must admit to you,
They never made a fuss.
And now with children of their own,
They're dreadful parents . . . just like us!

Olwyn Green

STOMP

Through the streets of the panic-stricken city stomped a beast,
Taller than the skyscrapers, from prehistory released;
Wreaking devastation, reducing all to rubble -
Tokyo, to put it mildly, was in deep trouble
As the monster swept aside every building with a swipe
Of its terrific claw and thrashing tail, of the lizard type.
The giant brute gave a fierce roar, then ploughed through
Whatever stood before it, because it wanted to.
Dust and smoke hung in clouds about its fearsome figure
While the behemoth continued to destroy with wanton vigour.
Great scales of emerald green adorned its hide like mail,
And frilled armoured plates jutted forth from top to tail;
Its clawed feet kicked aside the cars in its path,
Then stamped them to a mangled pulp to satisfy its wrath.
All the citizens had fled this nightmare scene for safer shores
Afraid they would finish up inside its mammoth jaws,
Leaving the city at the mercy of the creature -
If it didn't stomp upon you, rest assured it would eat ya!
This fiendishly enormous lizard smashed to pieces
Enough for an academic to write a thesis
On what that overgrown dinosaur thought it was doing
Marauding and lording it above Tokyo's ruin.
Then when seemingly there was nothing left to raze,
And the monster and the city could go their separate ways
A fleet of army tanks came rumbling into sight
Determined not to let the villain go without a fight.
Shells were set to be unleashed upon their beastly foe
But the prehistoric horror was prepared to lay them low
With a burst of fiery breath - when the director bellowed *'Cut!'*
And the actor in the rubber costume stayed put,
Till someone could assist him to climb out of his suit
So he could dine in the canteen before the afternoon shoot.

Jonathan Goodwin

THE ORDEAL

One night - with the toothache and stricken with pain!
I'd eaten a toffee. Oh, never again!
Hot drinks per pure torture; cold drinks hurt much more!
My jaw - it was aching, my gums were real sore!

So early next morning, the dentist I phoned,
To make an appointment; as I made it - I groaned!
'To get special treatment, come down in an hour!'
I wished it were sooner, until then I'd cower!

The time came, I entered - sat down in the chair;
As the dentist approached, I began to despair!
My mouth was examined, it was poked; it was pulled;
Would it be an extraction? That was soon overruled!

With a needle inserted, an injection was nigh!
In my wild imagination, I was sure I would die!
But my fears were allayed, as the 'freeze' took effect,
Soon my mouth was quite numb - was my dentist correct?

But the pain was not over, soon the drilling began!
In that room there was screaming! 'Twas the drill! Not me - man!
There was scraping and grinding and quite often, I'd wince!
When the drilling was over, the dentist said 'Rinse!'

Then there followed a silence, while amalgam was mixed,
In my tooth was inserted and that was it fixed!
'Have a final mouth rinse!' said the dentist, quite curt!
I was handed the bill and boy! Did that hurt!

But I cannot complain, I had lost my torment!
And the cash it had cost, was my money well spent!
So, if you should succumb, to incredible pain!
Give your dentist respect! And your teeth - he'll maintain!

Ron Bissett

THE MEETING

The desperate man glanced furtively round,
His gun in his holster gleaming,
Others regarded him but made no sound
To distract from his moody scheming.
He hadn't shaved for several days,
His chin was awash with stubble,
Dangerous when cornered, and sly in his ways
No one would dare burst his bubble.
A real desperado, or so it would seem,
A face from a wanted crime poster.
His eyes, mean and cruel, had a dangerous gleam,
The sign of a liar and boaster.
The sheriff sat near, assessing the scene,
A sardonic smile on his lips,
Watching and waiting, expectant and keen,
Making sure of no last minute slips.
An inquisitive fly buzzed irritatingly by,
The noise of its buzzing like thunder.
The law looked the other quite straight in the eye
Seeming ready to tear him asunder.
The whole seedy place had a desolate air,
Strange smells rent the air dank and queasy,
It reeked of false hope, and hopeless despair,
Where crime and bad-living were easy.
The man's lips curled in a terrible scowl,
The words were abrupt when they came,
'Bacon and eggs!' was the desperate growl,
And the sheriff said 'I'll have the same!'

Jack Scrafton

FROSTY WINDOWS

With every drop of crystal rain
That sparkled like diamanté
On the windowpane
Particles like glitz of glitterati

Gliding in frosted glare
Glaciated in a translucent
Glacial coated lair
Of icy compliment

Frosty crystals clinging
And sleigh bells ringing
Joyous cheer bringing
Jack Frost grinning

Cinderella in her slippers
Sloppy the seal flapping
With its flippers.

Ann Copland

THE AWAKENING

The first time I saw him my dislike was intense,
I'd never met him; it made little sense.
Since then I've seen him quite often but keep out of his way,
For I know without asking what he has to say.

Only the once I caught a glimpse of his eyes,
All I saw there were half-truths and lies.
His conscience was dimmed by the treasures he owned,
His tongue so sharp, his wit finely honed.

The God that he worshipped stood out on the drive,
Locked up in a bank, or due to arrive,
From funds invested in places offshore.
There would never be enough; he would always want more.

Who was this stranger, his face all blurred?
Something inside me was strangely disturbed.
At last the mist cleared, at last I could see.
I knew this stranger! This stranger was me!

WJFH

WHAT OF THE FUTURE?

What does the new millennium mean?
Is it a clear white sheet, or stars on beams?
Is it technology, robots, machines
Communicating by air waves, losing our dreams
Being swept along on this technical wave
Computerised brains that don't need to be brave

Our fathers and forefathers fought in wars
To give us a life, to open up doors
I am sure that they never dreamed
That the lives they saved would be electronically beamed!

Walk down any street in village or town
Are the children playing or walking, heads down
With a mobile 'phone attached to their ears?
Where is the laughter, the fun and the games?
What is the purpose, what are their aims?
Where are the marbles, hoops, hiding and seeking?
These children don't laugh they are only speaking
To someone not there but at the end of their 'phone
Is this then an age of being alone?

Are we in danger of losing ourselves
To the hi-tech equipment that sits on our shelves
We don't need discussion we just click, and enter!
Stare at a screen where from deep in the centre,
And *down load* the answers from *cyber space* teachers
What next, perhaps prayers from virtual preachers?

Discussion with peers, children, friends is the key
From these *hi-tech* chattels we need to break free
Not just using machines which may scramble the brain
And let's not forget that as good as they are
Machines came from people, a species greater by far!

Lynne M Hope

D I V O R C E

I'm sick of you
You're always there
No matter what I do
Please get a life
Move on, move out
Begin again anew.

By day, by night
I see you there
I'm never quite alone
I need my space
Do my own thing
My privacy is none.

So on your way
Get on yer bike
Clear off, please make it so,
For I don't love you anymore
My dearest own shad . . . ow!

Gerard Martin

THE PASSING OF TIME

The tigers have ripped your heart out,
The vultures have torn out your soul.
The eyes which shone, once, upon me,
Are empty, bottomless holes.

With you, life danced around us,
The gates of happiness ajar;
The velvet-smooth passage of time
Guided us there from afar.

But, time herself was an enemy
To the children who we were then;
While we, in our innocence, dawdled,
Lady Time, herself, wielded her pen.

Diamond eyes turned to marbles,
Fine physique now turned to dust,
Regretting our lost opportunities
In a world in which nothing seems just.

Twenty years of life for a kitten,
A good fifteen years for a dog;
For me, I can do naught but mourn
That for my pet I chose a frog.

Charlotte Dudley

ONLY LOVE CAN WIN

Kramer versus Kramer!
Two hearts perhaps,
Not quite at war.
They are just like
Beautiful Julie!
And Amy in May!
Two beautiful ladies,
I simply adore!
And then there's
Super Sheila!
So how can my love rest?
When each love
Is so lovely
When each love
Is the best!
Mitchell versus Mitchell!
How my head is in a spin!
But at least when
Love versus love!
Only love can win!

Graham Mitchell

A CARING COSHER

They'd lurked in the alleyway, week after week, to watch
                              Mr Percival Frank,
Arriving at seventeen-minutes-to-eight, deposit his cash in the bank;
'A creature of habit, our Percy,' said Sid, 'he's someone we know
                              we can trust -
It must be so hard when they're haphazard, like.' 'You're right,'
                              agreed Bertie, 'it must!'
The two would-be robbers, the young Herbert Snert, and veteran
                              thief, Sidney Snosh,
Had armed themselves suitably; Bert had a knife and Sid had a
                              good solid cosh:
They'd laid their plans carefully - here they were now, so stealthily
                              lying in wait
To take by surprise the old faithful cashier at seventeen-minutes
                              -to-eight.

They knew when the clock had chimed half-past the hour, the man
                              they were waiting to rob
Had balanced the books with meticulous care (old Percival
                              valued his job);
He'd open the safe where the money was kept and empty it into a sack
Then, carefully locking the premises up, would leave by the door
                              at the back.
They pictured him briskly beginning the walk that took seven minutes
                              in all -
He'd shortly appear with the small heavy sack to post in the safe
                              in the wall;
The robbers were tense with expectancy now: 'It's nearly the time,'
                              Sidney said,
'Remember to grab all the money as soon as I batter him on the head!'

Young Bertie said eagerly: 'I'll grab the cash and run down the road
                              for my life . . . '

'No, *Wait!*' replied Sid, 'he may struggle, you know, and then you
must plunge in the knife.'
'But Sid!' remarked Bertie, quite anxiously now 'I've never stabbed
anyone yet . . . '
' . . . If you want your share, then you'll do as I say - I'm running this
show, don't forget!'
The darkness had thickened; the clock struck the hour: 'He's late!'
complained old Sidney Snosh;
He moved around restlessly, shuffled about, and tested the weight
of his cosh:
'You don't suppose anything *happened* to him? I'm worried,' declared
Herbert Snert.
He tested his knife for its sharpness and said: 'I *do* hope he hasn't
been hurt!'

Rosemary Y Vandeldt

METAPHOR

That I am not, which I claim to be,
I am human that you would see,

I am two words, in that is a clue,
Yet I cannot half and become two,

It continually makes my life bliss,
Whenever I partake of this,

Leaves also play a part,
At the back I peek, at the front start,

My latter half would make you squirm,
So now you know I am a bookworm.

Ann G Wallace

THE CHRISTMAS RUSH

The Christmas rush has started and the cards are in the shops,
It makes me really wonder if the rushing ever stops,
Sweet muzak canned as carols is reverberating loud,
I bet if it was rock-and-roll it wouldn't be allowed.

Old Santa's in his Grotto, as the children queue with glee,
Three pounds a child with discount, if a mum has more than three.
There's holly round the checkout and a forest overhead
Of Christmas decorations in green and white and red.

The traffic queues are thickening and so are all the fumes
As Silent Night with anything but silence loudly booms;
The plastic slap of credit cards is added to the bills
As Christmas greeting shopping bags are bursting by the tills.

Bright Christmas lights are swinging in the silence of the sky
Adorning every tree or bush that dares to greet the eye;
A million 'Merry Christmases' are tinkling out a tune,
Which seems to me peculiar because it's only June!

Nicholas Winn

A FISHY TALE

My son and his family went out one day
To buy an aquarium and all its array
Pretty pond plants and ornaments too
And all the equipment as one must do.

One week later, his head in a whirl
He bought two fish, a boy and a girl
But the very next day to his surprise
She gave birth to sixteen right before his eyes.

The pet shop man said only a few would survive
But six weeks later they're all still alive
Getting bigger and stronger by the day
The tank looks quite full now, I must say.

But there is no end to this fishy game
Because today she did it again
My son exclaimed 'I can't cope with this
She's had another twenty fish.'

He only started with a pair
But now they're driving him to despair
So from this a lesson I can teach
When buying fish, don't get one of each.

Jean Cherrington

FORGIVE ME

My stomach sickens at the sight
of those significant remains,
broken and unadorned.

Nobody else was in the house
when it happened. Nobody else
to share the horror of my neglect.

I should have wrapped it in a bin liner,
obliterating it from sight,
but with social conscience I laid it

still warm, upon the cold
damp slab of concrete,
knowing the scavengers would come

and peck the slab clean.
But they let me down,
leaving fresh evidence for all to see.

He enters, eyes drawn immediately
to my crime and I cry out
please, forgive me.

His tears are my reply:
his birthday party is ruined
by that carelessly burnt cake.

Andrea Sandford

SHAGGY DOG STORY: A SESTINA

As he was walking with his dog
To brighten up a wintry spell,
A girl jogged past, and in no time
Emotion stirred his restless heart.
'Today,' he thought, 'I'll get it right -
This lonely life's gone on too long.'

With curly hair so sleek and long,
She trotted nimbly as his dog;
Outside the park, she then turned right.
Already underneath her spell
And hope now spurting in his heart,
He caught her up and asked the time.

'No watch,' she said. His pulse beat time
With her trim heels. She shrugged: 'So long!'
Dismissal cut him to the heart,
But luckily his friendly dog,
Tail-wagging, jumping, could dispel
Indifference and put things right.

They met for lunch. It was all right,
But he had not turned up on time.
Disaster this could surely spell:
Her face was looking rather long,
Until the antics of his dog
Quite made her choke on lettuce-heart.

He begged her be his own sweetheart:
Quick she declined - it was her right.
Would disappointment always dog
His path, rejected every time?
She left alone. How he did long
To write to her, but could not spell.

Her image he could not expel
From deep recesses of his heart.
She jogged the streets; he went along;
She thought his head was not quite right.
He did not see the bus in time . . .
It knocked him down. She claimed his dog.

So if you can't spell letters right,
And heart and mind don't work in time,
Your long-lost love may take your dog.

Anne Sanderson

SOMETHING THE VICAR SAID

She often wonders just why she stays
with a man who doesn't seem to care.
He never thanks her for meals she cooks,
for keeping the house and garden neat.
Not a cuddle, let alone a kiss
and never notices what she wears.

She just knew he wouldn't remember
her birthday, but it's no good to moan
or pity herself; too late for that.
She knew what she'd do tomorrow
and looked forward to her secret plan.
She's enjoy herself, all on her own.

A bus to town, a nice lunch perhaps
and a good look round all the big shops.
She'd buy herself something small and cheap
and be home in time to cook his meal.
She could guarantee without a doubt
he'd never suspect her little plot.

The other day much to her surprise
he agreed to go to church with her,
even though he left before the end.
She thought it was too good to be true.
She couldn't remember the last time
they'd been out for the night together.

Her plan in mind, she got up early
but he was up and dressed long before.
He said 'Sit down, I've made the tea,'
and she should open the gift wrapped box.
She found it hard to believe the man
perhaps still had something in store.

Flowers on the table, card and gift;
she must be dreaming, she couldn't speak!
The prettiest earrings, breakfast too.
'I've planned a special day for us,' and
what amazed her most, he did admit,
it was something the vicar said last week!

Mary Care

WALCOT

Gone are the old city walls
which kept the Clans of Holloway
and Walcot out.
Gone are the old city walls
for now we have the car to
zoom us about.
The Walacots want vehicles to
clog up the road,
but the Abbey dwellers are adamant:
they want the city walls.
The Walacots laughed at the monks
who came each day from St Catherine's
along the old Londinion Way.
They silently fished in the pond
now covered by North Parade
and picked apples from the orchard
during those endless summer days.
At night they met at the Burgh Mot
to sing and make merry
until prayers were begun.
The Walacots were angry because
they wouldn't buy their sheep:
so much wool and meat.
Instead, they invited the lepers and poor
to dine for a while on Christ Mass Day.

Tom Clarke

THE HOUSE UPON THE HILL

I thought a lot about the house, the house upon the hill
Walking by quite often, it looked so quiet and still
Windows broken, sagging down, the door stood drunkenly
No paint left on the woodwork, so sad for all to see

The garden looking rough and wild, a pond no longer there
An old swing broken on the ground, the lawn criss-crossed with brier
Most days my steps just carried me along the leafy lane
To the house upon the hill, time and time again

Long ago it seemed to me, as I stood and watched alone
Hearing laughter in my thoughts, this had been a happy home
Then one night I had a dream, at last my eyes could see
It was a place of elegance, I saw it differently

Very soon we bought the house, and started right away
With hammer, saw and paint brush, we worked both night and day
With windows shining brightly, new door a welcome sight
Children's laughter ringing through the rooms so clean and bright

The old front gate restored as new, the path swept fresh and clean
Flowers springing from the earth, that once could not be seen
I'm glad I walked so often to the house so quiet and still
And lived my dream of Heaven, in the house upon the hill

J Clifford